This book is dedicated to my daughter and my future grandkids.

-Tiffany Hollingsworth

Mommy has a baby in her belly!

A doula is a coach
who helps mommy
and my whole family.

Our doula reminds us
to cook colorful
and clean,
so you will grow strong
and mommy with stay healthy.

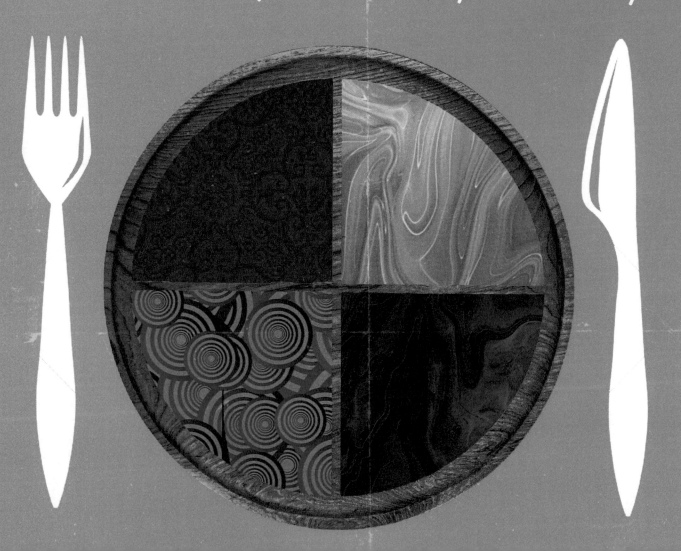

Our doula
tells mommy
to walk at least 4 miles
and check her blood
pressure everyday.

When our doula visits us,
we learn how to help mommy
relax, stretch, and breathe.

Daddy learns how to
lift mommy's belly
and rub her back
to relax her.

I tickle
mommy's feet
to make her laugh.

Mommy's doula
is my friend too!
I am going
to be a
big helper!

I have so many toys to share with you.

We are going to have so much fun together!

WELCOME HOME BABY !!!

When mommy and daddy
come home, our doula will visit us.
She helps mommy feed the baby
and helps daddy with chores.

Sometimes, she plays
dress up with me!!

Mommy gets tired
and cries sometimes.

Daddy and I remind Mommy that
she just had a baby and
it's normal to
feel overwhelmed sometimes.

Our doula checks in with
Mommy over the phone.
Sometimes they talk for hours!

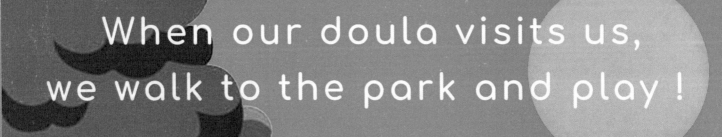

When our doula visits us,
we walk to the park and play !

While I play, Mommy
and our doula talk
and laugh alot.

Dear Parents & Caregivers,

Mommy Has A Doula© was written for Black pregnant and birthing people to start a conversation about what a doula is and how having a doula can benefit the entire family.

From grandparents to siblings alike, a doula can ease the stress of the unknown as we bring forth new life!

For more information about how a doula can help your growing family, go to www.simplyellen.org.

Thank you for supporting Black birthing families across the diaspora.

With every book sold, we pave the way for future generations to navigate pregnancy, birth, and parenting with joy!

Sincerely,

Ellen Branch-daughter of Tiffany & Anthony. Full Spectrum Doula, and owner of Simply Ellen Holistic Services LLC.

Simply Ellen

HOLISTIC SERVICES LLC